A Note to Parents

DK READERS is a compelling program for beginning readers, designed in conjunction with leading literacy experts, including Dr. Linda Gambrell, Director of the School of Education at Clemson University. Dr. Gambrell has served on the Board of Directors of the International Reading Association and as President of the National Reading Conference.

Beautiful illustrations and superb full-color photographs combine with engaging, easy-to-read stories to offer a fresh approach to each subject in the series. Each DK READER is guaranteed to capture a child's interest while developing his or her reading skills, general knowledge, and love of reading.

The four levels of DK READERS are aimed at different reading abilities, enabling you to choose the books that are exactly right for your child:

Level 1 – Beginning to read
Level 2 – Beginning to read alone
Level 3 – Reading alone
Level 4 – Proficient readers

The "normal" age at which a child begins to read can be anywhere from three to eight years old, so these levels are intended only as a general guideline.

No matter which level you select, you can be sure that you are helping your child learn to read, then read to learn!

LONDON, NEW YORK, MUNICH,
MELBOURNE, and DELHI

Project Editor Mary Atkinson
Art Editor Susan Calver
Senior Editor Linda Esposito
Deputy Managing Art Editor
Jane Horne
US Editor Regina Kahney
Production Kate Oliver
Picture Researcher Jo Carlill
Illustrator Norman Young

Reading Consultant
Linda B. Gambrell, Ph.D.

First American Edition, 1998
03 04 05 06 10 9 8 7 6 5 4
Published in the United States by DK Publishing, Inc.
375 Hudson Street, New York, New York 10014

Published in Great Britain by Dorling Kindersley Limited.

Library of Congress Cataloging-in-Publication Data
Nicholson, Sue.
    A Day at Greenhill Farm / by Sue Nicholson. --1st American ed.
    p.   cm. -- (Dorling Kindersley readers. Level 1)
    Summary: Introduces the animals on a farm – including the
chickens, ducks, cows, and pigs.
    ISBN 0-7894-2957-8
    1. Domestic animals--Juvenile literature. [1. Domestic animals.]
I. Title. II. Series.
SF75.5.N535   1998
636--DC21
                                            97-31285
                                                  CIP
                                                  AC
Color reproduction by Colourscan, Singapore
Printed and bound in China by L Rex Printing Co., Ltd.

The publisher would like to thank the following for
their kind permission to reproduce their photographs:
Key: t=top, b=below, l=left, r=right, c=center
Bruce Coleman Collection: 13tr, 13cr, 32clb;
Holt Studios International: Primrose Peacock 14bl; **Telegraph
Colour Library:** Thompson Studio Recording 14tl;
Tony Stone Images: 10tl.

Additional photography by Peter Anderson, Jon Bouchier,
Jane Burton, Peter Chadwick, Gordon Clayton, Philip Dowell,
Mike Dunning, Andreas Von Einsiedel, Dave King,
Bill Ling, Kim Taylor, and Barrie Watts.

All other images © Dorling Kindersley.
For further information see: www.dkimages.com

see our complete product line at

www.dk.com

DK READERS

BEGINNING TO READ 1

A Day at
Greenhill Farm

Written by Sue Nicholson

DK Publishing, Inc.

It is early in the morning.
The farm is quiet.

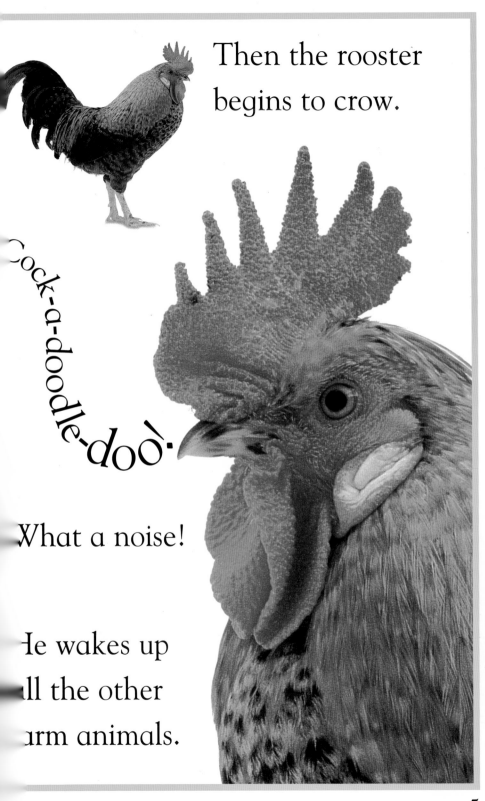

Then the rooster
begins to crow.

Cock-a-doodle-doo!

What a noise!

He wakes up
all the other
farm animals.

In the barn,
mother hen
starts to cluck.
One of her eggs
is ready
to hatch.

Cluck
Cluck

Peck, peck, peck!
A tiny chick breaks
through its shell.

More eggs crack open.
Five cheeping chicks
hatch out!

Cheep Cheep Cheep Cheep Cheep

Other farm babies
hatch from eggs too.

Quack
Quack

Mother duck has
six baby ducklings.

Mother goose
has four
baby goslings.

Honk
Honk

The ducks waddle
down to the pond.
They take
a morning dip.

Their wide,
webbed feet
push them
through the water.

The ducklings have soft, fluffy feathers called down.

down

Quack

Soon they will grow long, oily feathers to keep them warm and dry.

Geese like
to be near
water too.

Mother goose snaps up
grass and weeds
in her bright orange bill.

bill

Honk

She flaps her wings and honks
if anyone comes near
her goslings.

wing

The cows come
to the gate.
It is
milking time!

The farmer milks the cows.
He will sell the milk
for people to drink.

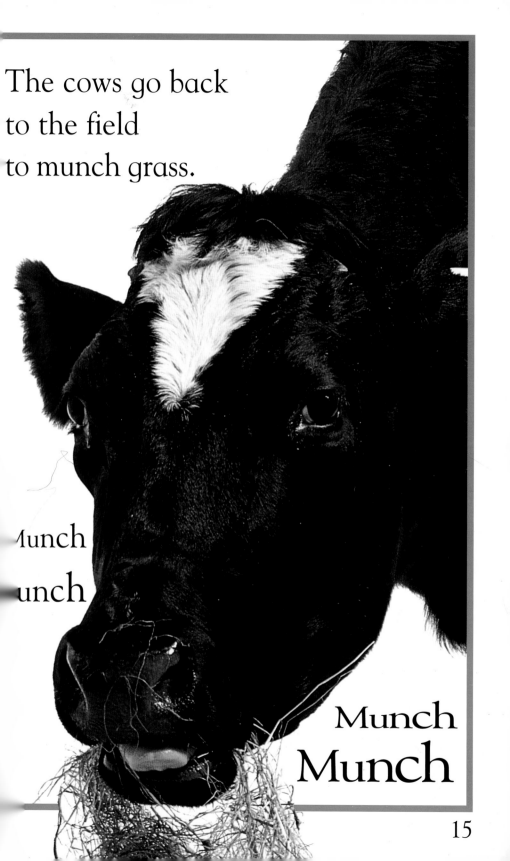

The cows go back
to the field
to munch grass.

Munch

unch

Munch

Munch

15

Other animals are hungry too.

A sheep
is nibbling hay.

So is a goat.

The pigs hunt
for food
in the barn.

One pig has her snout
in a bucket of corn!

snout

The farm babies
tell their mothers
that they are hungry.

"Baa, baa!" cries the lamb
to mother sheep.

Baa
Baa

"Naa, naa!" cries the kid
to mother goat.

Naa

Naa

The piglets squeal and squeak.
Then they drink their mother's milk.

There are lots of babies
on the farm.

The cat has kittens.

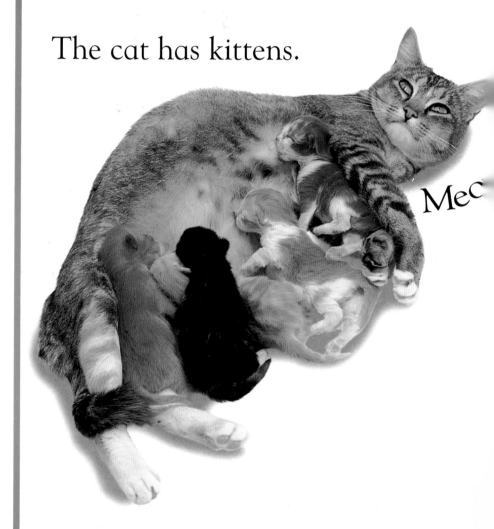

Mec

The kittens will grow up fast.

The mice
have babies too.

Squeak

Squeak

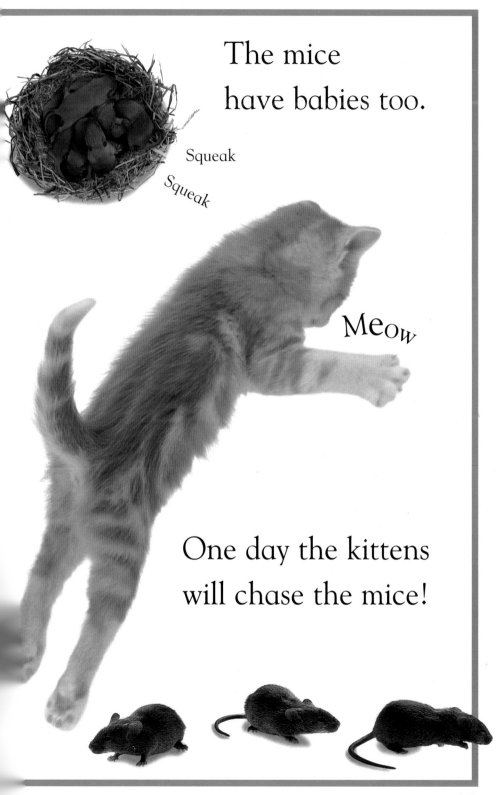

Meow

One day the kittens
will chase the mice!

Baby animals
love to play.

The kids butt each other
with their horns.

horns

The piglets
like to roll
in the mud.

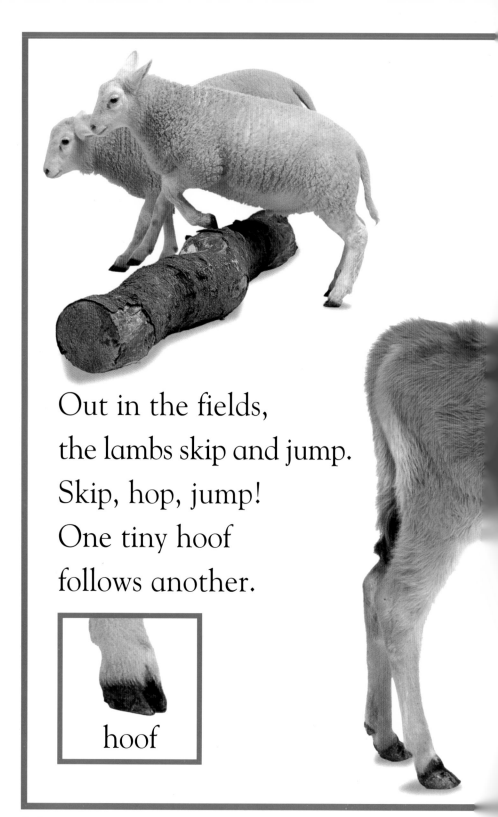

Out in the fields,
the lambs skip and jump.
Skip, hop, jump!
One tiny hoof
follows another.

hoof

One calf has lost his mother.
"Moo! Moo!" he calls.
The mother cow calls back.
She is not
far away.

Moo
Moo

Mother horse
has a baby foal.
He is only
two months old.
But he can run fast.

The foal races
around the field.
His mane blows
in the wind.

mane

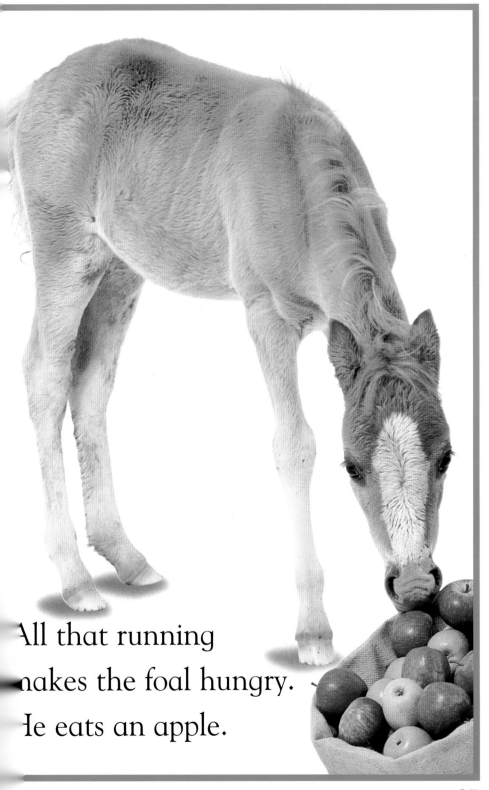

All that running
makes the foal hungry.
He eats an apple.

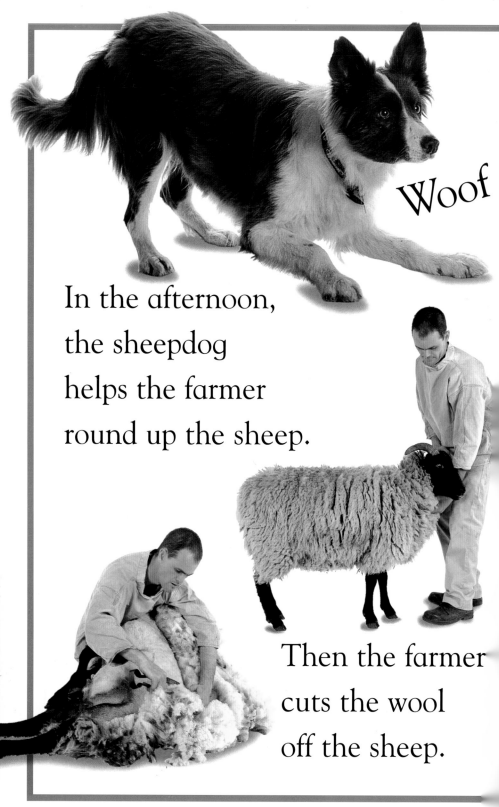

Woof

In the afternoon,
the sheepdog
helps the farmer
round up the sheep.

Then the farmer
cuts the wool
off the sheep.

The sheep look smaller and cleaner without their wool.

Baa
Baa

wool

Evening comes. It is dark.
The farm is quiet.

The chicks ...

and the lambs ...

Zzzzzzz

and the piglets fall fast asleep.

The cat will keep watch
until the rooster crows again.

Farm Vocabulary

down
page 11

horns
page 22

bill
page 12

hoof
page 24

wing
page 13

mane
page 26

snout
page 17

wool
page 2